Tiger Joy

Books by
STEPHEN *VINCENT BENÉT*

YOUNG ADVENTURE
HEAVENS AND EARTH
THE BEGINNING OF WISDOM
YOUNG PEOPLE'S PRIDE
JEAN HUGUENOT

Tiger Joy

A BOOK OF POEMS

BY

STEPHEN VINCENT BENÉT

"Oh, gentle Moon, thy crystal accents pierce
The caverns of my pride's deep universe
Charming the tiger, joy, . . .

PROMETHEUS UNBOUND.

NEW YORK
GEORGE H. DORAN COMPANY

TO ROSEMARY

If you were gone afar,
And lost the pattern
Of all your delightful ways,
And the web undone,
How would one make you anew,
From what dew and flowers,
What burning and mingled atoms,
Under the sun?

Not from too-satin roses,
Or those rare blossoms,
Orchids, scentless and precious
As precious stone.
But out of lemon-verbena,
Rose-geranium,
These alone.

Not with running horses,
Or Spanish cannon,
Organs, voiced like a lion,
Clamor and speed.
But perhaps with old music-boxes,
Young, tawny kittens,
Wild-strawberry-seed.

Even so, it were more
Than a god could compass
To fashion the body merely,
The lovely shroud.
But then—ah, how to recapture
That evanescence,
The fire that cried in pure crystal
Out of its cloud!

ACKNOWLEDGMENTS

Thanks are due to *The Bookman*, *The Century Magazine*, *The Literary Review*, *The Nation*, *The New Republic*, *The Saturday Review of Literature*, *The S4N*, and *Vanity Fair*, for permission to reprint poems included in this volume.

Special acknowledgment is made to E. Byrne Hackett and the Brick Row Book Shop for "The Ballad of William Sycamore," to Henry Holt and Company for permission to reprint "For All Blasphemers" from "The Beginning of Wisdom," and to The Yale University Press for permission to reprint "The Hemp" from "Young Adventure."

CONTENTS

[ix]

CONTENTS

[x]

I: FIDDLERS AND PIRATES

"And there be many fiddlers, eke, and
    pirates,
Whilk make a kind of horrid minstrelsy
Under the bloudy moon. Good wench,
    avoid them!"

The Tragedie of Tamar

THE BALLAD OF WILLIAM SYCAMORE

(1790—1871)

My father, he was a mountaineer,
His fist was a knotty hammer;
He was quick on his feet as a running deer,
And he spoke with a Yankee stammer.

My mother, she was merry and brave,
And so she came to her labor,
With a tall green fir for her doctor grave
And a stream for her comforting neighbor.

And some are wrapped in the linen fine,
And some like a godling's scion;
But I was cradled on twigs of pine
In the skin of a mountain lion.

And some remember a white, starched lap
And a ewer with silver handles;
But I remember a coonskin cap
And the smell of bayberry candles.

The cabin logs, with the bark still rough,
And my mother who laughed at trifles,
And the tall, lank visitors, brown as snuff,
With their long, straight squirrel-rifles.

I can hear them dance, like a foggy song,
Through the deepest one of my slumbers,
The fiddle squeaking the boots along
And my father calling the numbers.

The quick feet shaking the puncheon-floor,
And the fiddle squealing and squealing,
Till the dried herbs rattled above the door
And the dust went up to the ceiling.

There are children lucky from dawn till dusk,
But never a child so lucky!
For I cut my teeth on "Money Musk"
In the Bloody Ground of Kentucky!

When I grew tall as the Indian corn,
My father had little to lend me,
But he gave me his great, old powder-horn
And his woodsman's skill to befriend me.

With a leather shirt to cover my back,
And a redskin nose to unravel

[14]

Each forest sign, I carried my pack
As far as a scout could travel.

Till I lost my boyhood and found my wife,
A girl like a Salem clipper!
A woman straight as a hunting-knife
With eyes as bright as the Dipper!

We cleared our camp where the buffalo feed,
Unheard-of streams were our flagons;
And I sowed my sons like the apple-seed
On the trail of the Western wagons.

They were right, tight boys, never sulky or slow,
A fruitful, a goodly muster.
The eldest died at the Alamo.
The youngest fell with Custer.

The letter that told it burned my hand.
Yet we smiled and said, "So be it!"
But I could not live when they fenced the land,
For it broke my heart to see it.

I saddled a red, unbroken colt
And rode him into the day there;
And he threw me down like a thunderbolt
And rolled on me as I lay there.

The hunter's whistle hummed in my ear
As the city-men tried to move me,
And I died in my boots like a pioneer
With the whole wide sky above me.

Now I lie in the heart of the fat, black soil,
Like the seed of a prairie-thistle;
It has washed my bones with honey and oil
And picked them clean as a whistle.

And my youth returns, like the rains of Spring,
And my sons, like the wild-geese flying;
And I lie and hear the meadow-lark sing
And have much content in my dying.

Go play with the towns you have built of blocks,
The towns where you would have bound me!
I sleep in my earth like a tired fox,
And my buffalo have found me.

THE HEMP

(A Virginia Legend)

THE PLANTING OF THE HEMP

Captain Hawk scourged clean the seas
(Black is the gap below the plank)
From the Great North Bank to the Caribbees.
(Down by the marsh the hemp grows rank).

His fear was on the seaport towns,
The weight of his hand held hard the downs.

And the merchants cursed him, bitter and black,
For a red flame in the sea-fog's wrack
Was all of their ships that might come back.

For all he had one word alone,
One clod of dirt in their faces thrown,
"The hemp that shall hang me is not grown!"

His name bestrode the seas like Death,
The waters trembled at his breath.

This is the tale of how he fell,
Of the long sweep and the heavy swell,
And the rope that dragged him down to hell.

[18]

The fight was done, and the gutted ship,
Stripped like a shark the sea-gulls strip,

Lurched blindly, eaten out with flame,
Back to the land from whence she came,
A skimming horror, an eyeless shame.

And Hawk stood up on his quarter-deck,
And saw the sky and saw the wreck.

Below, a butt for sailors' jeers,
White as the sky when a white squall nears,
Huddled the crowd of the prisoners.

Over the bridge of the tottering plank,
Where the sea shook and the gulf yawned blank,
They shrieked and struggled and dropped and sank.

Pinioned arms and hands bound fast.
One girl alone was left at last.

Sir Henry Gaunt was a mighty lord.
He sat in state at the Council board.

The governors were as naught to him.
From one rim to the other rim

Of his great plantations, flung out wide
Like a purple cloak, was a full month's ride.

Life and death in his white hands lay,
And his only daughter stood at bay,
Trapped like a hare in the toils that day.

He sat at wine in his gold and his lace,
And far away, in a bloody place,
Hawk came near, and she covered her face.

He rode in the fields, and the hunt was brave,
And far away, his daughter gave
A shriek that the seas cried out to hear,
And he could not see and he could not save.

Her white soul withered in the mire
As paper shrivels up in fire,
And Hawk laughed, and he kissed her mouth,
And her body he took for his desire.

THE GROWING OF THE HEMP

Sir Henry stood in the manor room,
And his eyes were hard gems in the gloom.

And he said, "Go, dig me furrows five
Where the green marsh creeps like a thing alive—
There at its edge where the rushes thrive."

And where the furrows rent the ground
He sowed the seed of hemp around.

And the blacks shrink back and are sore afraid
At the furrows five that rib the glade,
And the voodoo work of the master's spade.

For a cold wind blows from the marshland near,
And white things move, and the night grows drear,
And they chatter and crouch and are sick with fear.

But down by the marsh, where the grey slaves glean,
The hemp sprouts up, and the earth is seen
Veiled with a tenuous mist of green.

And Hawk still scourges the Caribbees,
And many men kneel at his knees.

Sir Henry sits in his house alone,
And his eyes are hard and dull like stone.

And the waves beat, and the winds roar,
And all things are as they were before.

And the days pass, and the weeks pass,
And nothing changes but the grass.

But down where the fireflies are like eyes,
And the damps shudder, and the mists rise,
The hemp-stalks stand up toward the skies.

And down from the poop of the pirate ship
A body falls, and the great sharks grip.

Innocent, lovely, go in grace!
At last there is peace upon your face.

And Hawk laughs loud as the corpse is thrown,
"The hemp that shall hang me is not grown!"

Sir Henry's face is iron to mark,
And he gazes ever in the dark.

And the days pass, and the weeks pass,
And the world is as it always was.

[22]

But down by the marsh the sickles gleam,
Glitter on glitter, gleam on gleam,
And the hemp falls down by the stagnant stream.

And Hawk beats up from the Caribbees,
Swooping to pounce in the Northern seas.

Sir Henry sits sunk deep in his chair,
And white as his hand is grown his hair.

And the days pass, and the weeks pass,
And the sands roll from the hour-glass.

But down by the marsh, in the blazing sun,
The hemp is smoothed and twisted and spun.
The rope made, and the work done.

THE USING OF THE HEMP

Captain Hawk scourged clean the seas,
(Black is the gap below the plank)
From the Great North Bank to the Caribbees
(Down by the marsh the hemp grows rank)

He sailed in the broad Atlantic track
And the ships that saw him came not back.

Till once again, where the wide tides ran,
He stopped to harry a merchantman.

He bade her stop.   Ten guns spake true
From her hidden ports, and a hidden crew,
Lacking his great ship through and through.

Dazed and dumb with the sudden death,
He scarce had time to draw a breath

Before the grappling-irons bit deep
And the boarders slew his crew like sheep.

Hawk stood up straight, his breast to the steel;
His cutlass made a bloody wheel.

[24]

His cutlass made a wheel of flame.
They shrank before him as he came.

And the bodies fell in a choking crowd,
And still he thundered out aloud,

"The hemp that shall hang me is not grown!"
They fled at last.   He was left alone.

Before his foe Sir Henry stood.
"The hemp is grown and my word made good!"

And the cutlass clanged with a hissing whir
On the lashing blade of the rapier.

Hawk roared and charged like a maddened buck.
As the cobra strikes, Sir Henry struck,

Pouring his life in a single thrust,
And the cutlass shivered to sparks and dust.

Sir Henry stood on the blood-stained deck,
And set his foot on his foe's neck.

Then, from the hatch, where the torn decks slope,
Where the dead roll and the wounded grope,
He dragged the serpent of the rope.

The sky was blue and the sea was still,
The waves lapped softly, hill on hill,
And between one wave and another wave
The doomed man's cries were little and shrill.

The sea was blue and the sky was calm,
The air dripped with a golden balm.
Like a wind-blown fruit between sea and sun,
A black thing writhed at a yard-arm.

Slowly then, and awesomely,
The ship sank, and the gallows-tree,
And there was nought between sea and sun—
Nought but the sun and the sky and the sea.

But down by the marsh, where the fever breeds,
Only the water chuckles and pleads;
For the hemp clings fast to a dead man's throat,
And blind Fate gathers back her seeds.

THE MOUNTAIN WHIPPOORWILL

(*Or, How Hill-Billy Jim Won the Great Fiddlers' Prize*)

(*A Georgia Romance*)

Up in the mountains, it's lonesome all the time,
(Sof' win' slewin' thu' the sweet-potato vine.)

Up in the mountains, it's lonesome for a child,
(Whippoorwills a-callin' when the sap runs wild).

Up in the mountains, mountains in the fog,
Everythin's as lazy as an old houn' dog.

Born in the mountains, never raised a pet,
Don't want nuthin' an' never got it yet.

Born in the mountains, lonesome-born,
Raised runnin' ragged thu' the cockleburrs and corn.

Never knew my pappy, mebbe never should.
Think he was a fiddle made of mountain laurel-wood.

Never had a mammy to teach me pretty-please.
Think she was a whippoorwill, a-skitin' thu' the
    trees.

Never had a brother ner a whole pair of pants,
But when I start to fiddle, why, yuh got to start to
dance!

*Listen to my fiddle—Kingdom Come—Kingdom
Come!*
Hear the frogs a-chunkin' "Jug o' rum, Jug o' rum!"
*Hear that mountain-whippoorwill be lonesome in
the air,*
*An' I'll tell yuh how I travelled to the Essex County
Fair.*

Essex County has a mighty pretty fair,
All the smarty fiddlers from the South come there.

Elbows flyin' as they rosin up the bow
For the First Prize Contest in the Georgia Fiddlers'
Show.

Old Dan Wheeling, with his whiskers in his ears,
King-pin fiddler for nearly twenty years.

Big Tom Sargent, with his blue wall-eye,
An' Little Jimmy Weezer that can make a fiddle cry.

All sittin' roun', spittin' high an' struttin' proud,
*(Listen, little whipporwill, yuh better bug yore
eyes!)*

Tun-a-tun-a-tunin' while the jedges told the crowd
Them that got the mostest claps'd win the bestest
prize.

Everybody waitin' for the first tweedle-dee,
When in comes a-stumblin'—hill-billy me!

Bowed right pretty to the jedges an' the rest,
Took a silver dollar from a hole inside my vest,

Plunked it on the table an' said, "There's my callin'
card!"
"An' anyone that licks me—well, he's got to fiddle
hard!"

Old Dan Wheeling, he was laughin' fit to holler,
Little Jimmy Weezer said, "There's one dead
dollar!"

Big Tom Sargent had a yaller-toothy grin,
But I tucked my little whippoorwill spang under-
neath my chin,
An' petted it an' tuned it till the jedges said,
"Begin!"

Big Tom Sargent was the first in line;
He could fiddle all the bugs off a sweet-potato-vine.

He could fiddle down a possum from a mile-high
    tree.
He could fiddle up a whale from the bottom of the
    sea.

Yuh could hear hands spankin' till they spanked
    each other raw,
When he finished variations on "Turkey in the
    Straw".

Little Jimmy Weezer was the next to play;
He could fiddle all night, he could fiddle all day.

He could fiddle chills, he could fiddle fever,
He could make a fiddle rustle like a lowland river.

He could make a fiddle croon like a lovin' woman.
An' they clapped like thunder when he'd finished
    strummin'.

Then came the ruck of the bob-tailed fiddlers,
The let's-go-easies, the fair-to-middlers.

They got their claps an' they lost their bicker,
An' settled back for some more corn-licker.

An' the crowd was tired of their no-count squealing,
When out in the center steps Old Dan Wheeling.

He fiddled high and he fiddled low,
(Listen, little whippoorwill, yuh got to spread yore
wings!)
He fiddled with a cherrywood bow.
(Old Dan Wheeling's got bee-honey in his strings).

He fiddled the wind by the lonesome moon,
He fiddled a most almighty tune.

He started fiddling like a ghost,
He ended fiddling like a host.

He fiddled north an' he fiddled south,
He fiddled the heart right out of yore mouth.

He fiddled here an' he fiddled there.
He fiddled salvation everywhere.

When he was finished, the crowd cut loose,
(Whippoorwill, they's rain on yore breast.)
An' I sat there wonderin' "What's the use?"
(Whippoorwill, fly home to yore nest.)

But I stood up pert an' I took my bow,
An' my fiddle went to my shoulder, so.

An'—they wasn't no crowd to get me fazed—
But I was alone where I was raised.

[31]

Up in the mountains, so still it makes yuh skeered.
Where God lies sleepin' in his big white beard.

An' I heard the sound of the squirrel in the pine,
An' I heard the earth a-breathin' thu' the long night-
    time.

They've fiddled the rose, an' they've fiddled the
    thorn,
But they haven't fiddled the mountain-corn.

They've fiddled sinful an' fiddled moral,
But they haven't fiddled the breshwood-laurel.

They've fiddled loud, and' they've fiddled still,
But they haven't fiddled the whippoorwill.

I started off with a *dump-diddle-dump*,
(Oh, hell's broke loose in Georgia!)
Skunk-cabbage growin' by the bee-gum stump,
(Whippoorwill, yo're singin' now!)

Oh, Georgia booze is mighty fine booze,
The best yuh ever poured yuh,
But it eats the soles right offen yore shoes,
For Hell's broke loose in Georgia.

My mother was a whippoorwill pert,
My father, he was lazy,
But I'm hell broke loose in a new store shirt
To fiddle all Georgia crazy.

Swing yore partners—up an' down the middle!
Sashay now—oh, listen to that fiddle!
Flapjacks flippin' on a red-hot griddle,
An' hell broke loose,
Hell broke loose,
Fire on the mountains—snakes in the grass.
Satan's here a-bilin'—oh, Lordy, let him pass!
Go down Moses, set my people free,
Pop goes the weasel thu' the old Red Sea!
Jonah sittin' on a hickory-bough,
Up jumps a whale—an' where's yore prophet now?
Rabbit in the pea-patch, possum in the pot,
Try an' stop my fiddle, now my fiddle's gettin' hot!
Whippoorwill, singin' thu' the mountain hush,
Whippoorwill, shoutin' from the burnin' bush,
Whippoorwill, cryin' in the stable-door,
Sing tonight as yuh never sang before!
Hell's broke loose like a stompin' mountain-shoat,
Sing till yuh bust the gold in yore throat!
Hell's broke loose for forty miles aroun'

Bound to stop yore music if yuh don't sing it down.
Sing on the mountains, little whippoorwill,
Sing to the valleys, an' slap 'em with a hill,
For I'm struttin' high as an eagle's quill,
An' Hell's broke loose,
Hell's broke loose,
Hell's broke loose in Georgia!

They wasn't a sound when I stopped bowin',
(*Whippoorwill, yuh can sing no more.*)
But, somewhere or other, the dawn was growin',
(*Oh, mountain whippoorwill!*)

An' I thought, "I've fiddled all night an' lost.
"Yo're a good hill-billy, but yuh've been bossed."

So I went to congratulate old man Dan,
—But he put his fiddle into my han'—
An' then the noise of the crowd began.

MOON-ISLAND

(Deposition of Christopher Hew, the Last American Pirate)

1.

When we first sighted land
How it made our hearts thunder
To think of new plunder
Dropped into our hand!
When we first sighted land.

It was Midsummer Day
When we let go the anchor,
But the sun had no rancor
Within that calm bay.

We rowed to its shores
With our muskets beside us
And a devil to ride us
With red-hot moidores.

But the beach was so white,
And the slow minutes crept,

And the hot devil slept,
And the moon rose, in light,

Frail as nautilus shell,
And somehow—in our souls—
We forgot we were coals
Half-rejected by hell.

We had come there to loot,
But we sprawled and grew tame there.
And brown women came there
With baskets of fruit.

Fruit cold as moonshine
With a strange taste, and sweet,
With a taste that could beat
Any Portugal wine.

They kept singing a tune,
And we ate—and we gaped—
For each fruitseed was shaped
Like a little new moon.

2.

Then we drowsed without care
For our devil was gone,
And the singing kept on,
And the moon filled the air.

And we did not go back
To our ship in the bay,
To our old bird of prey
Where the Roger flapped slack,
And we had the arrack.

No, we lingered and stayed,
And time passed like the sleep
Yellow emperors keep
In their coffins of jade,

While we swam in the pool
Or we played knucklebones
Or we skipped little stones
Like boys out of school.

By the gold hands of day
And the silver of night
We were coins scoured bright
And our sins fell away.

We were wasps without stings,
We were children again there.
Oh, we could have been men there!
We could have been kings.

3.

On the last night of all
The moon was at full,
And we heard the tide pull
At the beach's pale shawl.

And the moonseeds had grown
As the moon grew in size,
Till like round silver eyes
In the dark fruit they shone.

And we ate, and the tune
That the brown women sang
Gathered and rang
In a heathenish croon,

As we tossed out the seeds
For the moonbeams to bleach
On the long, burnished beach
Like a goddess's beads.

And then—was it a dream
Or the wine of the fruit?
The moonseeds took root
Where the light made them gleam.

And the roots grew and swelled
And were quickened to vine
In the opal-bright shine,
And we, gasping, beheld

A great Moonvine of pearl
Burgeon under our eyes.
And we saw it arise,
And we saw it uncurl,

An ivory fret,
A glittering stair
Of cold crystal and air,
And the end was not yet.

The brown women's tune
Chanted deeper and deeper.
We saw the pearl creeper
Lay hold of the Moon!

Then the wild song was ended
And we held our breath.
And, in silence like death,
The White Moon descended.

And first she was far
As Heaven is far.

And then she was far
As mortal things are.

And first she was round
And then ghostly with pearl,
And then she was a girl
And stepped to the ground.

She was milk of the pearl.
She was naked as light.
She was fire in the night,
White fire of the pearl.
And—she was a girl.

4.

Then the women, light-drowned,
Knelt, covering their eyes,
And the radiant skies
Gave a clear, silver sound.

When someone—not I—
No—not I—but some other—
I swear it! Oh Mother
Of Mercies, not I!

Came crawling the track
Of an Indian asp

With a gun in his clasp
Behind her white back.

There was sand in the pan,
And the priming was damp.
And she burned like a lamp.
But he was a man.

Like hoarfrost she shined,
Like new sails in the sun,
But he raised the clubbed gun
And struck—from behind.
And then we were blind.

5.

There was not a sound.
There was not a spark.
But we lay on the ground
Like bones in the dark.

In a darkness more black
Than ebony-stone,
We lay there alone
And felt our hearts crack.

Till the dawn rose in blood
And we rose without speech,

And we saw that the beach
Was the color of blood.

And we got to our boat
Without speech, and gave way
For the ship, where she lay
Like a dead man afloat.

And we got the sails set
And went out with the wind.
And the isle fell behind
But we could not forget.

How could we forget,
When we lay down to rest,
And Night bared her black breast,
And no moon rose or set?

The night came too soon.
We could live, in the sun.
But it sank and was done,
And there was not a moon.
There was never a moon.

Only darkness, clay-cold
As a snake, sucking strength—
When you caught us at length
We were madmen grown old.

But my madness is gone,
And I know where I've been.
I know what I've seen,
And I know when I'm done.

Tell Kidd to move over
His brimstone-and-rum,
For we'll be the clover
Of Hell when we come.

You hangman of tailors,
Here's Satan's doubloon!
Silk rope for the sailors
That murdered the Moon!

II: SILVER AND GOLD

"Under the thorn is hunger and cold,
Under the broom is silver and gold."

CHEMICAL ANALYSIS

She's slender hands and pretty lips,
And seafoam and rosemary.
Her ears are pointed at the tips,
She stayed so long in Fairy.

NOMENCLATURE

Some people have names like pitchforks, some people
    have names like cakes,
Names full of sizzling esses like a family quarrel of
    snakes,
Names black as a cat, vermilion as the cockscomb-hat
    of a fool—
But your name is a green, small garden, a rush
    asleep in a pool.

When God looked at the diffident cherubs and
    dropped them out of the sky,
He named them like Adam's animals, while Mary
    and Eve stood by,
The poor things huddled before him in scared little
    naked flocks
—And he gave you a name like sunlight, and clover,
    and hollyhocks.

For your mouth with its puzzled jesting, for your
    hair like a dark soft bird,
Shy humor and dainty walking, sweet laughter and
    subtle word,

As a fairy walks with a mushroom to keep the rain
    from its things
You carry your name forever, like a sceptre alive
    with wings.

Neither change nor despair shall touch it nor the
    seasons make it uncouth,
It will burn like an Autumn maple when your proud
    age talks to your youth,
Wise child, clean friend, adoration, light arrow of
    God, white flame,
I would break my body to pieces to call you once by
    your name!

DIFFERENCE

My mind's a map.   A mad sea-captain drew it
Under a flowing moon until he knew it;
Winds with brass trumpets, puffy-cheeked as jugs,
And states bright-patterned like Arabian rugs.
"Here there be tygers."   "Here we buried Jim."
Here is the strait where eyeless fishes swim
About their buried idol, drowned so cold
He weeps away his eyes in salt and gold.
A country like the dark side of the moon,
A cider-apple country, harsh and boon,
A country savage as a chestnut-rind,
A land of hungry sorcerers.

                                  Your mind?

—Your mind is water through an April night,
A cherry-branch, plume-feathery with its white,
A lavender as fragrant as your words,
A room where Peace and Honor talk like birds,
Sewing bright coins upon the tragic cloth
Of heavy Fate, and Mockery, like a moth,

Flutters and beats about those lovely things.
You are the soul, enchanted with its wings,
The single voice that raises up the dead
To shake the pride of angels.

                         I have said.

A SAD SONG

Rosemary, Rosemary,
There's a Pig in your garden,
With silk bristles frizzy
And tushers of snow!
But Rosemary was cautious,
She said, "Beg your pardon!
I'm really too busy
To look down below."

Rosemary, Rosemary,
There's a Bird in your kitchen!
His voice is gold water,
He says, 'Pretty Poll!'
But Rosemary heard nothing,
Putting stitch after stitch in
The dress of a daughter,
Her thirty-sixth doll.

Rosemary, Rosemary,
A silver-winged Rabbit!

He bridles and gentles
And wants you astride!
"I prefer," said Rosemary,
"To ride a Good Habit."
She went buying black lentils—
She did till she died.

A NONSENSE SONG

Rosemary, Rosemary, let down your hair!
The cow's in the hammock, the crow's in the chair!
I was making you songs out of sawdust and silk,
But they came in to call and they spilt them like
    milk.

The cat's in the coffee, the wind's in the east,
He screams like a peacock and whines like a priest
And the saw of his voice makes my blood turn to
    mice—
So let down your long hair and shut off his advice!

Pluck out the thin hairpins and let the waves stream,
Brown-gold as brook-waters that dance through a
    dream,
Gentle-curled as young cloudlings, sweet-fragrant
    as bay,
Till it takes all the fierceness of living away.

Oh, when you are with me, my heart is white steel.
But the bat's in the belfry, the mold's in the meal,
And I think I hear skeletons climbing the stair!
—Rosemary, Rosemary, let down your bright hair!

TO ROSEMARY, ON THE METHODS BY WHICH SHE MIGHT BECOME AN ANGEL

Not where the sober sisters, grave as willows,
Walk like old twilights by the jasper sea,
Nor where the plump hunt of cherubs holly-hilloes
Chasing their ruddy fox, the sun, you'll be!

Not with the stained-glass prophets, bearded grimly,
Not with the fledgling saved, meek Wisdom's lot,
Kissing a silver book that glimmers dimly,
For acolytes are mild and you are not.

They'll give you a curled tuba, tall as Rumor,
They'll sit you on a puff of Autumn cloud,
Gilded-fantastic as your scorn and humor
And let you blow that tuba much too loud.

Against the unceasing chant to sinless Zion,
Three impudent seraph notes, three starry coals,
Sweet as wild grass and happy as a lion
—And all the saints will throw you aureoles.

EVENING AND MORNING

Over the roof, like burnished men,
The stars tramp high.
You blink—the fire blinks back again
With a cock's red eye.
Lay your book away to doze,
Say your silly prayers,
See that nothing grabs your toes
And run upstairs!

Sandman eyes and heavy head,
Sleep comes soon,
Pouring on your quiet bed
The great, cool moon.
Nod's green wheel of moss turns round,
Dripping dreams and peace,
Gentle as a pigeon's sound,
Soft as fleece.

Think of warm sheep shuffling home,
Stones sunk deep,
Bees inside a honeycomb—
Sleep—Sleep.

[56]

Smile as when young Una smiled,
Hard and sweet and gay,
Bitter saint, fantastic child,
Fold your wings away.

Dawn, the owl, is fluttering
At Day's bright bars.
Night, the lame man, puttering,
Puffs out the stars.
Wake! and hear an airy shout
Crack the egg of cloud,
And see the golden bird creep out,
Ruffling and proud.

IN A GLASS OF WATER BEFORE RETIRING

Now the day
Burns away.
Most austere
Night is here
—Time for sleep.

And, to sleep,
If you please,
For release
Into peace,
Think of these.

Snails that creep,
Silver-slow;
Streams that flow,
Murmuring,
Murmuring;
Bells that chime,
Sweet—clear—c-o-o-l;
Of a pool
Hushed so still

Stars drowse there,
Sleepy-fair;
Of a hill
Drenched with night,
Drowned with moon's
Lovely light;
Of soft tunes,
Played so slow,
Kind and low,
You sink down,
Into down,
Into rest,
Into the perfect whiteness,
The drowsy, drowsy lightness,
The warm, clean, sleepy feathers of a slum-
bering bird's white breast.

LEGEND

The trees were sugared like wedding-cake
With a bright, hoar frost, with a very cold snow,
When we went begging for Jesus' sake,
Penniless children, years ago.

Diamond weather—but nothing to eat
In that fine, bleak bubble of earth and skies.
Nothing alive in the windy street
But two young children with hungry eyes.

"We must go begging or we will die.
I would sell my soul for an apple-core!"
So we went mendicant, you and I,
Knock-knock-knock at each snow-choked door.

Knock-knock-knock till our fingers froze.
Nobody even replied "Good day!",
Only the magistrate, toasting his toes,
Howled at us sleepily, "Go away!"

"Rosemary dear, what shall we do?"
"Stephen, I know not.   Beseech some saint!
My nose has turned to an icicle blue,
And my belly within me is very faint."

"If there be saints, they are fast asleep,
Lounging in Heaven, in wraps of feather."
"Talk not so, or my eyes will weep
Till the ice-tears rattle and clink together."

"Saints are many—on which shall I call?
He must be kindly, without constraint."
"I think you had better pray to Saint Paul.
I have heard people call him a neighborly saint."

Down he flopped on his cold, bare knees
—Breath that smoked in the bitter air—
Crossing his body with hands afreeze,
He sought Saint Paul in a vehement prayer.

Scarce had these shiverers piped "Amen,"
Cheeping like fledglings, crying for bread,
When good Saint Paul appeared to them then,
With a wide gold halo around his head.

He waved his episcopal hand, and smiled,
And the ground was spread like a banquet-table!
"Here is much good food for each hungry child,
And I hope you will eat as long as you're able."

"Here are good, thick cloaks for your ragged backs,
And strong, warm boots for your feet," said he,

"And for Stephen, gloves and a little axe,
And a little fur muff for Rosemary."

They thanked him humbly, saying a Pater,
Before they had touched a morsel even,
But he said, "Your thanks are for One far greater"
And pointed his right arm up at Heaven.

"For you are the sparrows around God's door,
He will lift you up like His own great banner.
But the folk who made you suffer so sore—
He shall deal with them in another manner.

"It is His own will to transport those folk
To a region of infinite ice and snow."
And his breath was a taper of incense-smoke,
And he lifted a finger—and it was so.

And the folk were gone—and the saint was fled—
And we stared and stared at the wintry land.
And in front of us there was a banquet spread.
And a little fur-muff on Rosemary's hand.

DULCE RIDENTEM

The bee, he has white honey,
The Sunday child her muff,
The rich man lots of money
Though never quite enough,
The apple has a Springtime smell,
The star-fields silver grain,
But I have youth, the cockleshell,
And the sweet laugh of Jane.

The lark's tune goes so clearly
But Jane's is clear wells.
The cuckoo's voice currs cheerly,
But Jane's is new bells.
Whether she chuckles like a dove,
Or laughs like April rain,
It is her heart and hands and love,
The moth-wing soul of Jane.

ALL NIGHT LONG

We were in bed by nine, but she did not hear the
    clock,
She lay in her quiet first sleep, soft-breathing, head
    by her arm,
And the rising, radiant moon spilled silver out of
    its crock
On her hair and forehead and eyes as we rested,
    gentle and warm.

All night long it remained, that calm, compassionate
    sheet,
All the long night it wrapped us in whiteness like
    ermine-fur,
I did not sleep all the night, but lay, with wings
    on my feet,
Still, the cool at my lips, seeing her, worshipping her.

Oh, the bright sparks of dawn when day broke,
    burning and wild!
Oh, the first waking glance from her sleepy, beau-
    tiful eyes!
With a heart and a mind newborn as a naked,
    young, golden child,
I took her into my arms. We saw the morning arise!

DAYS PASS: MEN PASS

When, like all liberal girls and boys,
We too get rid of sight
—The juggler with his painted toys
The elf and her delight—

In the cool place where jests are few
And there's no time to weep
For all the untamed hearts we knew
Creeping like moths to sleep.

This eagerness that burns us yet
Will rot like summer snow,
And we'll forget as winds forget
When they have ceased to blow.

Oh, we'll grow sleepy, lacking mirth!
But there will still endure
Somewhere, like innocence and earth,
The things your wish made pure.

Wide moonlight on a harvest dew,
White silk, too dear to touch,
These will be you and always you
When I am nothing much.

The flowers with the hardy eyes,
The bread that feeds the gods,
These will be you till Last Assize
When I'm improper sods.

Oh dear immortal, while you can,
Commit one mortal sin.
And let me love you like a man
Till Judgment Day comes in!

III: KING DAVID

KING DAVID

David sang to his hook-nosed harp:
"The Lord God is a jealous God!
His violent vengeance is swift and sharp!
And the Lord is King above all gods!

"Blest be the Lord, through years untold,
The Lord Who has blessed me a thousand fold!

"Cattle and concubines, corn and hives
Enough to last me a dozen lives.

"Plump, good women with noses flat,
Marrowful blessings, weighty and fat.

"I wax in His peace like a pious gourd,
The Lord God is a pleasant God,
Break mine enemy's jaw, O Lord!
For the Lord is King above all gods!"

His hand dropped slack from the tunable strings,
A sorrow came on him—a sorrow of kings.

A sorrow sat on the arm of his throne,
An eagle sorrow with claws of stone.

[69]

"I am merry, yes, when I am not thinking,
But life is nothing but eating and drinking.

"I can shape my psalms like daggers of jade,
But they do not shine like the first I made.

"I can harry the heathen from North to South,
But no hot taste comes into my mouth.

"My wives are comely as long-haired goats,
But I would not care if they cut their throats!

"Where are the maids of the desert tents
With lips like flagons of frankincense?

"Where is Jonathan? Where is Saul?
The captain-towers of Zion wall?

"The trees of cedar, the hills of Nod,
The kings, the running lions of God?

"Their words were a writing in golden dust,
Their names are myrrh in the mouths of the just.

"The sword of the slayer could never divide them—
Would God I had died in battle beside them!"

The Lord looked down from a thunder-clap.
(The Lord God is a crafty God.)
He heard the strings of the shrewd harp snap.
(The Lord Who is King above all gods.)

He pricked the king with an airy thorn,
It burnt in his body like grapes of scorn.

The eyelids roused that had drooped like lead.
David lifted his heavy head.

The thorn stung at him, a fiery bee,
"The world is wide. I will go and see
From the roof of my haughty palace," said he.

II.

Bathsheba bathed on her vine-decked roof.
(The Lord God is a mighty God.)
Her body glittered like mail of proof.
(And the Lord is King above all gods.)

Her body shimmered, tender and white
As the flesh of aloes in candlelight.

King David forgot to be old or wise.
He spied on her bathing with sultry eyes.

A breath of spice came into his nose.
He said, "Her breasts are like two young roes."

His eyes were bright with a crafty gleam.
He thought, "Her body is soft as cream."

He straightened himself like an unbent bow
And called a servant and bade him go.

III.

Uriah the Hittite came to his lord,
Dusty with war as a well-used sword.

A close, trim man like a belt, well-buckled;
A jealous gentleman, hard to cuckold.

David entreated him, soft and bland,
Offered him comfits from his own hand.

Drank with him deep till his eyes grew red,
And laughed in his beard as he went to bed.

The days slipped by without hurry or strife,
Like apple-parings under a knife,
And still Uriah kept from his wife.

Lean fear tittered through David's psalm,
"This merry husband is far too calm."

David sent for Uriah then,
They greeted each other like pious men.

"Thou hast borne the battle, the dust and the heat.
Go down to thy house and wash thy feet!"

Uriah frowned at the words of the king.
His brisk, hard voice had a leaden ring.

"While the hosts of God still camp in the field
My house to me is a garden sealed.

"How shall I rest while the arrow yet flies?
The dust of the war is still in my eyes."

David spoke with his lion's roar:
"If Peace be a bridle that rubs you sore,
You shall fill your belly with blood and war!"

Uriah departed, calling him kind.
His eyes were serpents in David's mind.

He summoned a captain, a pliable man,
"Uriah the Hittite shall lead the van.

"In the next assault, when the fight roars high,
And the Lord God is a hostile God,
Retire from Uriah that he may die.
For the Lord is King above all gods."

IV.

The messenger came while King David played
The friskiest ditty ever made.

"News, O King, from our dubious war!
The Lord of Hosts hath prevailed once more!

[73]

"His foes are scattered like chirping sparrows,
Their kings lie breathless, feathered with arrows.

"Many are dead of your captains tall.
Uriah the Hittite was first to fall."

David turned from the frolicsome strings
And rent his clothes for the death of kings.

Yet, as he rent them, he smiled for joy.
The sly, wide smile of a wicked boy.

"The powerful grace of the Lord prevails!
He has cracked Uriah between His nails!

"His blessings are mighty, they shall not cease.
And my days henceforth shall be days of peace!"

His mind grew tranquil, smoother than fleece.
He rubbed his body with scented grease.
And his days thenceforward were days of peace.

His days were fair as the flowering lime
—For a little time, for a little time.

And Bathsheba lay in his breast like a dove,
A vessel of amber, made for love.

V.

When Bathsheba was great with child,
(The Lord God is a jealous God!)
Portly and meek as a moon grown mild,
(The Lord is King above all gods!)

Nathan, the prophet, wry and dying,
Preached to the king like a locust crying:

"Hearken awhile to a doleful thing!
There were two men in thy land, O King!

"One was rich as a gilded ram.
One had one treasure, a poor ewe-lamb.

"Rich man wasted his wealth like spittle.
Poor man shared with his lamb spare victual.

"A traveler came to the rich man's door.
'Give me to eat, for I hunger sore!'

"Rich man feasted him fatly, true,
But the meat that he gave him was fiend's meat, too,
Stolen and roasted, the poor man's ewe!

"Hearken, my lord, to a deadly thing!
What shall be done with these men, O King?"

[75]

David hearkened, seeing it plain,
His heart grew heavy with angry pain:
"Show me the rich man that he be slain!"

Nathan barked as a jackal can.
"Just, O King! And thou art the man!"

David rose as the thunders rise
When someone in Heaven is telling lies.
But his eyes were weaker than Nathan's eyes.

His huge bulk shivered like quaking sod,
Shoulders bowing to Nathan's rod,
Nathan, the bitter apple of God.

His great voice shook like a runner's, spent,
"My sin has found me! Oh, I repent!"

Answered Nathan, that talkative Jew:
"For many great services, comely and true,
The Lord of Mercy will pardon you.

"But the child in Bathsheba, come of your seed,
Shall sicken and die like a blasted weed."

David groaned when he heard him speak.
The painful tears ran hot on his cheek.

[76]

Ashes he cast on his kingly locks.
All night long he lay on the rocks.

Beseeching his Lord with a howling cry:
"O Lord God, O my jealous God,
Be kind to the child that it may not die,
For Thou art King above all gods!"

VI.

Seven long nights he lay there, howling,
A lion wounded, moaning and growling.

Seven long midnights, sorrowing greatly,
While Sin, like a dead man, embraced him straitly.

Till he was abased from his lust and pride
And the child was born and sickened and died.

He arose at last.   It was ruddy Day.
And his sin like water had washed away.

He cleansed and anointed, took fresh apparel,
And worshiped the Lord in a tuneful carol.

His servants, bearing the child to bury,
Marveled greatly to see him so merry.

He spoke to them mildly as mid-May weather:
"The child and my sin are perished together.

"He is dead, my son. Though his whole soul yearn
    to me,
I must go to him, he may not return to me.

"Why should I sorrow for what was pain?
A cherished grief is an iron chain."

He took up his harp, the sage old chief.
His heart felt clean as a new green leaf.

His soul smelt pleasant as rain-wet clover.
"I have sinned and repented and that's all over.

"In his dealings with heathen, the Lord is hard.
But the humble soul is his spikenard."

His wise thoughts fluttered like doves in the air.
"I wonder is Bathsheba still so fair?

"Does she weep for the child that our sin made
    perish?
I must comfort my ewe-lamb, comfort and cherish.

"The justice of God is honey and balm.
I will soothe her heart with a little psalm."

He went to her chamber, no longer sad,
Walking as light as a shepherd lad.

He found her weeping, her garments rent,
Trodden like straw by God's punishment.
He solaced her out of his great content.

Being but woman, a while she grieved,
But at last she was comforted, and conceived.

Nine months later she bore him a son.
(The Lord God is a mighty God!)
The name of that child was SOLOMON.
He was God's tough staff till his days were run!
(And the Lord is King above all gods!)

IV: STICKS AND STONES

"Sticks and stones may break your bones,
Cross words will never hurt you."

EPITAPH

Grapes that a hand strips down a vine,
Dice that an idle wrist has flung,
The wind blows off true friends of mine—
Some are dead, some married young.

FOR ALL BLASPHEMERS

Adam was my grandfather,
A tall, spoiled child,
A red, clay tower
In Eden, green and mild.
He ripped the Sinful Pippin
From its sanctimonious limb.
Adam was my grandfather—
And I take after him.

Noah was my uncle
And he got dead drunk.
There were planets in his liquor-can
And lizards in his bunk.
He fell into the Bottomless
Past Hell's most shrinking star.
Old Aunt Fate has often said
How much alike we are.

Lilith, she's my sweetheart
Till my heartstrings break,
Most of her is honey-pale

And all of her is snake.
Sweet as secret thievery,
I kiss her all I can,
While Somebody Above remarks
"That's not a nice young man!"

Bacchus was my brother,
Nimrod is my friend.
All of them have talked to me
On how such courses end.
But when His Worship takes me up
How can I fare but well?
For who in gaudy Hell will care?
—And I shall be in Hell.

LOST

With a start I arose where the moon waved pale
    on my bed—
For the night rang out to a clamor like desolate gulls,
To the pallid dispute of the chittering souls of the
    dead
Wizenedly seething afar in a river of skulls.

And "We are betrayed!" said one, and "Eternity
Is lost! Eternity's lost!" in the voice of dim rain,
And the twilight of answering shadows took up the
    cry
"Eternity's lost!" and they rustled like leaves again.

I shuddered and crept to the warmth and the idle
    dream,
But through all the long stupor of night they
    quavered at me,
Wailing like withered-up reeds in the drought of
    a stream,
Crying like birds for forgotten Eternity.

[86]

ARCHITECTS

My son has built a fortified house
To keep his pride from the thunder,
And his steadfast heart from the gnawing mouse
That nibbles the roots of wonder.

My daughter's wit has hammered and filed
Her slight and glittering armor.
She hides in its rings like a dragon-child,
And nothing on earth can harm her.

My wife has molded a coffin of lead
From the counterfeit tears of mourners.
She rests in it, calm as a saint long dead,
And the Four Winds kneel at its corners.

I have scooped my den with a crafty thumb
In the guts of an arid acre.
And it may not last till Kingdom Come
—But it will not cripple its maker.

It is six feet long by three feet deep
And some may call it narrow.
But, when I get into it, I can keep
The nakedness of an arrow.

THE GOLDEN CORPSE

(Eight Sonnets for Donald Malcolm Campbell)

1.

Stripped country, shrunken as a beggar's heart,
Inviolate landscape, hardened into steel,
Where the cold soil shatters under heel
Day after day like armor cracked apart.

Winter Connecticut, whose air is clean
As a new icicle to cut the throat,
Whose black and rigid trees will not demean
Themselves to swagger in a crystal coat.

I hate you as a bastard hates his name
When your cramped hills are hostile with the white,
But, every year, when March comes in the same,
A frozen river rolling in the night,

I must go back and hunt among your snow
Something I lost there, much too long ago.

[88]

2.

It was not innocence, it was not scorn,
And yet it had these names and many more.
It was a champion blowing on a horn,
It was the running of a golden boar.

It was a stallion, trampling the skies
To rags of lightning with his glittering shoes,
It was a childish god with lazy eyes,
It was an indolent and reckless Muse.

More than all these, it was a spirit apart,
Purely of fire and air and the mind.
No fear could eat the temper from its heart
Nor any fleshly bandage make it blind.

It was a silver dagger in the blast.
It was the first of youth, and it has passed.

3.

I left it in a bare and windy street
Between two sets of bells whose casual chimes
Answer each other, janglingly and sweet,
Like the concord of long-repeated rhymes.

I left it in a since-demolished bar,
And underneath a rain-streaked paving-stone.
And, men and things being what they are,
The hidden ghost had better couch alone.

I shall not rattle with an iron fist
The relics, scattered into sticks of chalk,
Of what was once the carcass of a hawk
That sat like Wrath on an archangel's wrist.

Nor disinter, to make my house look smart,
That thunder-broken and ferocious heart.

4.

Men that dig up a mandrake know dis-ease.
This body is committed to its bones
Down where the taproots of New England trees
Suck bare existence from the broken stones.

All summer cannot quicken it with heat,
Nor Spring perturb it with a budding bough,
Nor all the glittering devils of the sleet
In snowing Winter rack its quiet now.

But, in October, when the apples fall,
And leaves begin to rust before the cold,
There may occur, by some unnoticed wall,
A sigh, a whisper in the rotten gold.

A breath that hardly can be called a breath
From Death that will not yet acknowledge Death.

5.

Unnoticed—for the years have hardier tasks
Than listening to a whisper or a sigh.
They creep among us with a bag of masks
And fit them to our brows obsequiously.

Some are of iron, to affront the gay,
And some of bronze, to satirize the brave,
But most are merely a compost of clay
Cut in the sleepy features of a slave.

With such astuteness do they counterfeit,
We do not realize the masks are on
Till, gaudy in our folly, bit by bit
We notice that a neighbor's face seems drawn.

And then, with fingers turned to lumps of stone,
Touch the inhuman cast that was our own.

6.

There is no doubt such workmanship is sage.
The bound and ordered skies could not abide
A creature formed of elemental rage
For longer than a moment of its pride.

The hand that stooped to Adam from the cloud
And touched his members with a fiery spine
Designed as well the pattern of the shroud
That should convince him he was not divine.

And there are sorceries more excellent
Than the first conflagration of the dust,
But none are quite so single in intent
Or unsophisticated with distrust.

The ripened fruit is golden to the core
But an enchantment fosters it no more.

7.

Therefore, in neither anguish nor relief,
I offer to the shadow in the air
No image of a monumental grief
To mock its transience from a stony chair,

Nor any tablets edged in rusty black.
Only a branch of maple, gathered high
When the crisp air first tastes of applejack,
And the blue smokes of Autumn stain the sky.

A branch whose leaves cling to the withering staff
Like precious toys of gilt and scarlet paint,
An emblem Life and Death share half-and-half,
A brittle sceptre for a dying saint.

Unburning fire, an insubstantial Host,
A violence dreamt, a beauty of the ghost.

8.

So much in memory.   For the future, this.
The checkerboarded house of Day and Night
Is but a cavern where a swallow flies
To beat its wings an instant at the light

And then depart, where the incessant storm
Shepherds the planets like a drunken nurse.
It does not need an everlasting form
To dignify an ecstasy so terse.

But while the swallow fluttered and was quick
I have marked down its passage in the dark
And charred its image on a broken stick
With the brief flame of an uncertain spark.

The fire can have it now, the rain can rain on it,
And the ice harden like a god's disdain on it.

SNOWFALL

Heaven is hell, if it be as they say,
All endless day.
A pen of terrible radiance, on whose walls
No shadow falls,
No sunset ever comes because no sun has ever risen,
Where, like bewildered flies,
Poor immortalities
Interminably crawl, caught in a crystal prison.

Yet, if there is but night to recompense
Impertinence,
How can we bear to live so long and know
The end is so?
Creatures that hate the dark, to utmost dark
          descending?
The worm's dull enmity,
To feel it—but not see!
To be afraid at night and know that night unending!

There is a time when, though the sun be weak,
It is not bleak
With perfect and intolerable light,
Nor has the night

Yet put those eyes to sleep that do not wish for
    slumber;
When, on the city we know,
The pale, transmuting snow
Falls softly, in sighing flakes, immaculate, without
    number.

Whisperingly it drifts, and whisperingly
Fills earth and sky
With fragile petals, tranquil as a swan's
Blanch pinions.
And where it falls is silence, subtle and mild.
That silence is not cruel
But calm as a frozen jewel,
And clasped to its cold frail breast Earth sucks in
    rest like a child.

If there can be a heaven, let it wear
Even such an air.
Not shamed with sun nor black without a ray,
But gently day.
A tired street, whereon the snow falls, whitely,
An infant, cradled in fleece,
An ancient, drowsy with peace,
Unutterable peace, too pure to shine too brightly.

CAROL: NEW STYLE

If Jesus Christ should come again,
On Christmas day, on Christmas day,
To bother the minds of gentlemen
On Christmas day in the morning?

The first one said as he passed by,
As he passed by, as he passed by,
"I see three thieves a-hanging high,
This Christmas day in the morning."

The second one said, "What sinful men!
What sinful men, what sinful men!
Hanging is too good for them,
On Christmas day in the morning."

The third one said, "Oh stay your word!
Stay your word, oh stay your word!
Do you not see that one's the Lord,
This Christmas day in the morning?"

"I know him by his weary head,
His weary head, his weary head."

Whereat they all fell sore adread,
That Christmas day in the morning.

"How sad this is we all avow,
Yes indeed, we all avow!
But what shall we do about it now,
On Christmas day in the morning?"

Primus
"I'll run away as fast as I may,
As fast as I may, as fast as I may,
And pretend I haven't been out all day,
On Christmas day in the morning."

Secundus
"I'll buy Him a shroud that's spick and span,
Spick and span, spick and span,
For I was always a generous man,
On Christmas day in the morning."

Tertius
"But what if we should cut Him down,
Cut Him down, cut Him down?"

Secundus et Primus
"You fool, do you want to arouse the town,
On Christmas day in the morning?"

"My speech was rash," the third one said,
The third one said, the third one said,
"We're surer of God when we know He's dead,
On any day in the morning."

They knelt in the snow and prayed and bowed,
Prayed and bowed, prayed and bowed,
And the two dead thieves laughed out aloud
On Christmas day in the morning.

As Jesus Christ was hanging high,
Hanging high, hanging high,
He saw three Christians, passing by,
On Christmas day in the morning.

X-RAY

Smile if you will or frown, wear silk or serge,
Play age or youth, it will not help, my dear.
This is a place where Truth is made too clear
For idle minds to watch that Truth emerge.
The penetration of this light is just,
Inhuman, and most mercilessly pure.
From its assault upon your house of dust
Only the naked scaffold will endure.

Beneath the perfect candor of this ray
All mortal comeliness lies overthrown,
And even human blood is merely grey,
And ribs and joints are beautiful alone
As the weak flesh contests but cannot stay
The passionless search for the eternal bone.

UNFAMILIAR QUARTET

The concert-hall creaked like a full-dress shirt
As the happy audience hugged its musical smart,
And waited to be titillatingly hurt
By the pelting of the over-ripe fruit of Art.

The violin wept its sugar, the saxophone
Howled like a mandrake raped by a lightning-stroke,
The cello gave a blond and stomachy groan—
And then the hard bugle spoke.

Sewing a wound together with brazen stitches,
Stitching a bronze device on the rotten skin,
And calling the elegant audience sons of bitches,
It ceased, and the sons of bitches
Applauded the violin.

AZRAEL'S BAR

He stood behind the counter, mixing drinks,
Pride for the old, who like their liquor tart,
Green scorn *frappé* to cheer the sick-at-heart,
False joy, as merry as a bed of pinks.

He had the eyes of a sarcastic lynx
And in his apron was a small black dart
With which he stirred, secretive and apart,
His shaker, till it rang with poisonous clinks.

I fumbled for the rail.   "The same, with gin?
Love—triple star—you like the velvet kick?"
I shook with the blind agues of the sick.
Then, through lost worlds, his voice, *"Fini,* old
    friend?"
He poured black drops out, cold as dead men's skin:
"So?   This is what we always recommend——"

HEART'S BLOOD

Others can offer you the courtly red
That lies in veins just underneath the skin
Which may be fathomed with a silver pin
That leaves no scar to show the flesh has bled.
And others still, that deep, arterial flood
Dark as wood-violets sodden in the rain.
That gift is rare but may be given again.
I have a different taste, in giving blood.

Take up the cup. It will not dye your hand
With pretty little threads of scarlet waste
Or purples that can have a counterpart.
Yet, it has virtues—for I understand
Such clotted liquor is not brewed in haste
And can be got from nowhere but the heart.

WORMS' EPIC

Because all little green things love the sun
They let us travel.
               Slow as moving sand,
Crawling as babies crawl across the floor,
Half-drowning when we burst a drop of dew,
All our new bodies tender with too much light,
We crept out of the rose's burning heart
To a curled petal, paused, and looked about
With fragile, timid eyes at the huge world.

But we were most exploring and untamed
And hardy. When the time had come to fly
We felt a silver shiver in our hearts
Like listening to thunder, and the shock
Cold harpstrings feel under the thrilling hand,
And over us, although we could not see,
Knew the long, delicate, gauzy wings unfold.
Hearts hot as candleflame, eyes wicked with mirth,
We threw ourselves upon the immense, bright air.

What earthquakes and adventures fell on us
In that first second! Mayhem, piracy,

Black murder, featherfoot loving like the touch
Of light on wings, of moon upon the snow!
And through it all the crystal of our flight,
One clear, continual thread.
       A dragonfly
Zoomed over us like a bombing aeroplane,
And we were terrified to death.
        A bird
Snapped up our seven best friends in one quick snatch
And left us shivering.
       A gigantic toad
Gazed at us with great eyes like Arctic moons
And nearly made us goblins.
        And the sun,
That incandescence heavy in the air,
Moved in us like warm sea-water, wave and wave.
And through it all our crystal flight—and love—

The change came.   The sky deepened like an eye.
Twilight, the shadowy child, vague as blown smoke,
Called all her furry bats out of their sleep
And ran with them across the darkening fields.

Now we return, tired with the happy day,
And tired with something drowsier than that,